# There W
# a Princess
# Long Ago

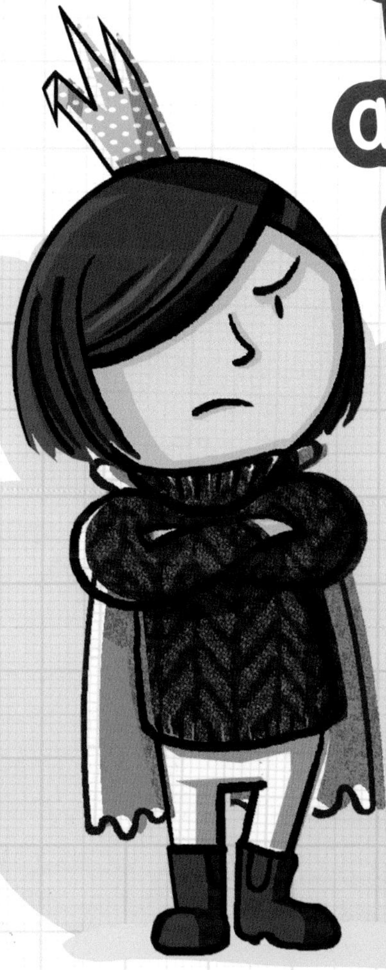

Story by Alison Hawes
Illustrated by Garry Parsons

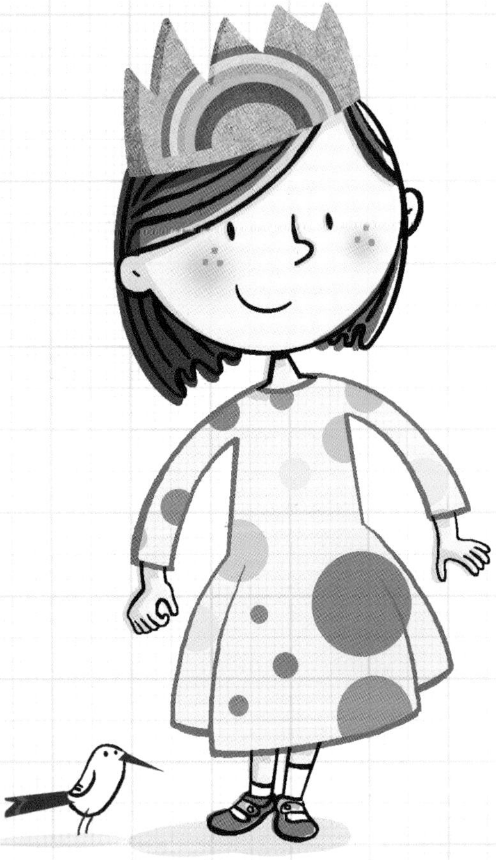

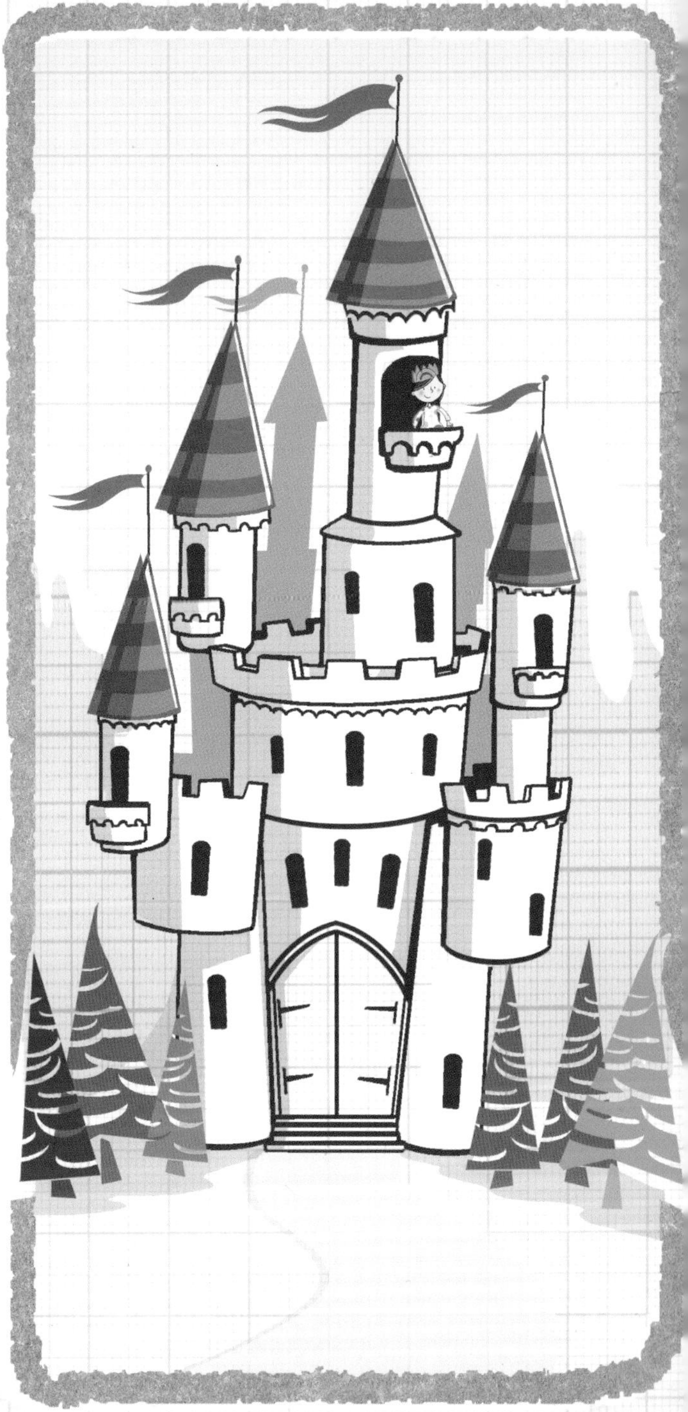

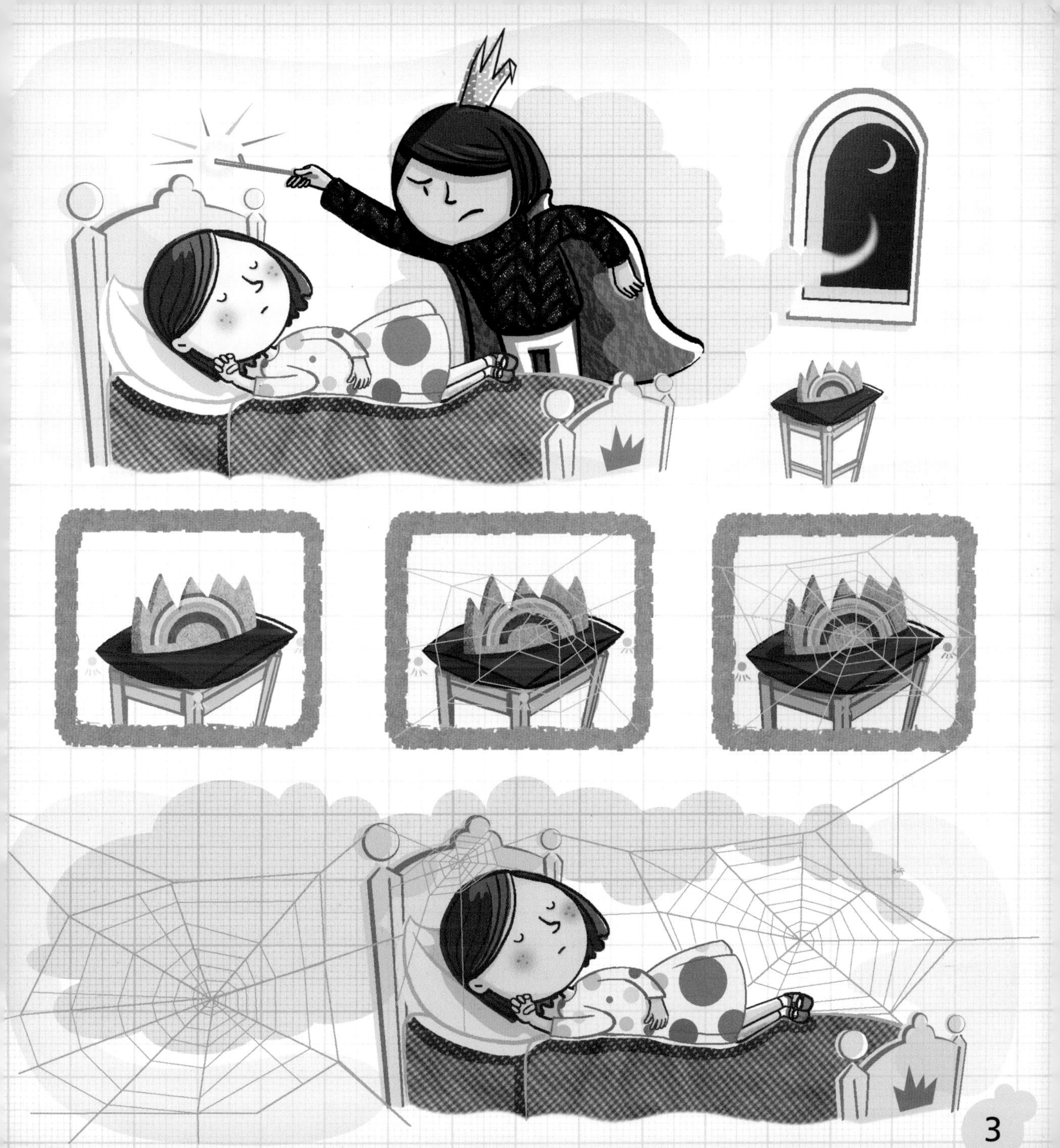

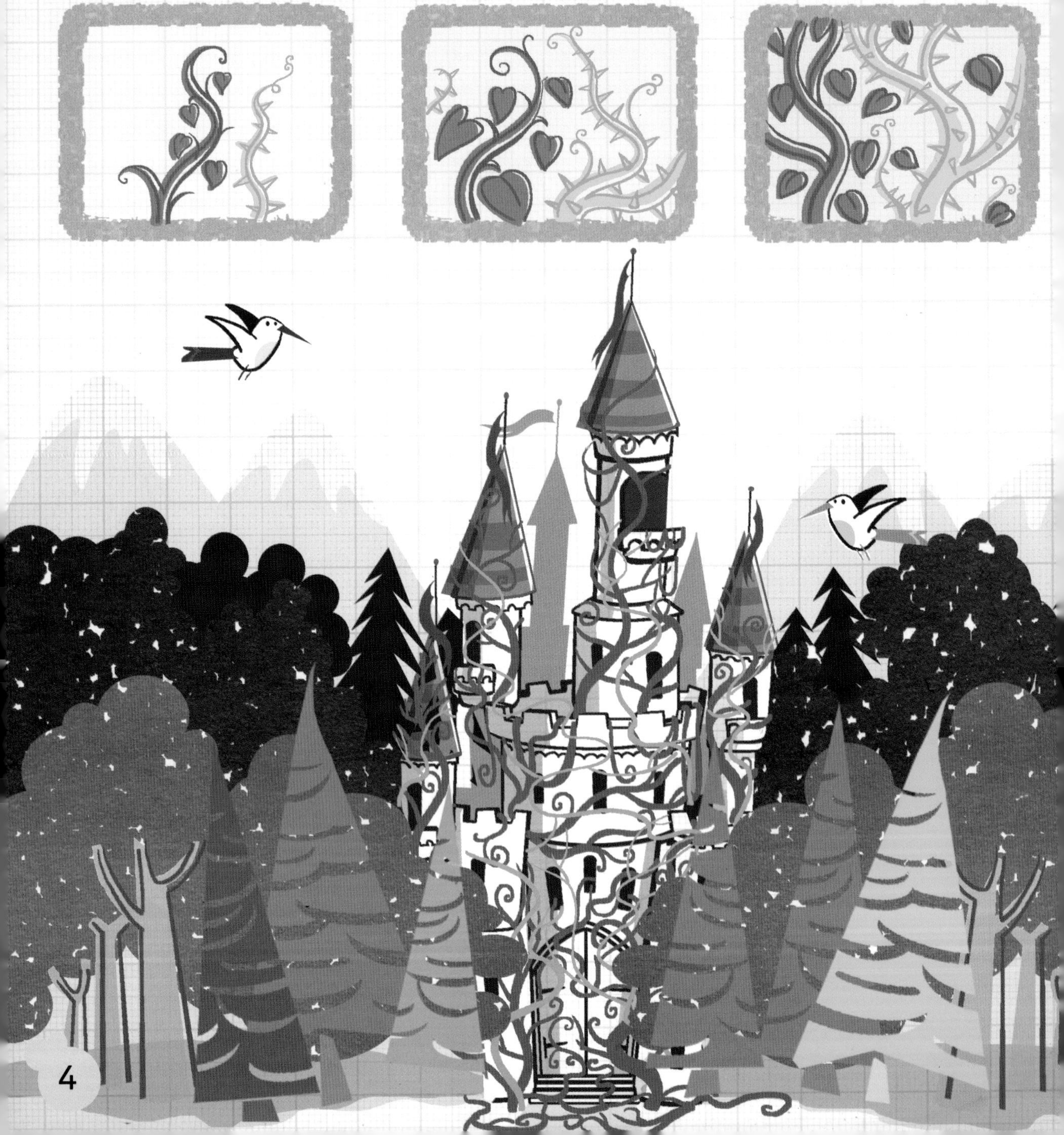

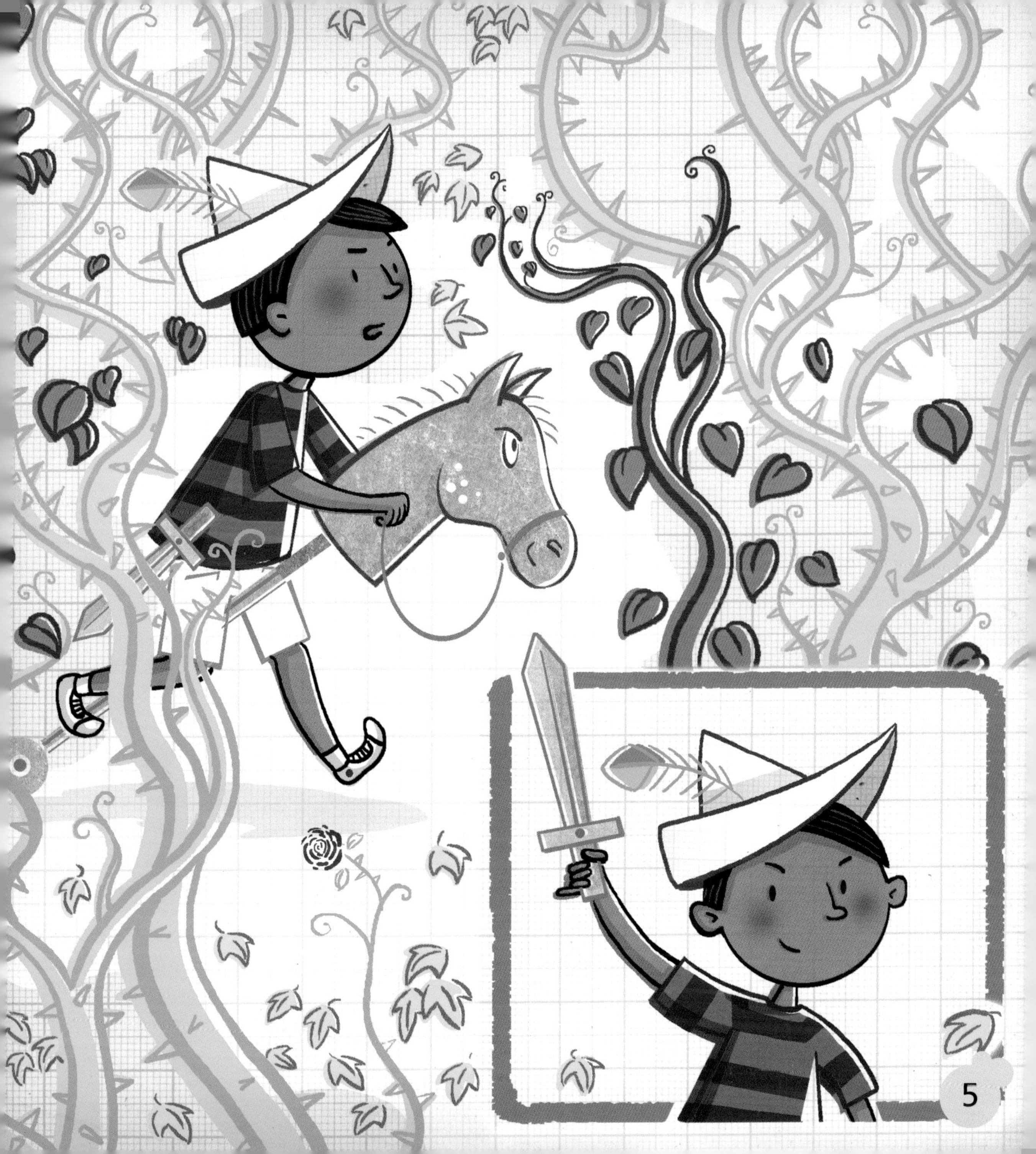

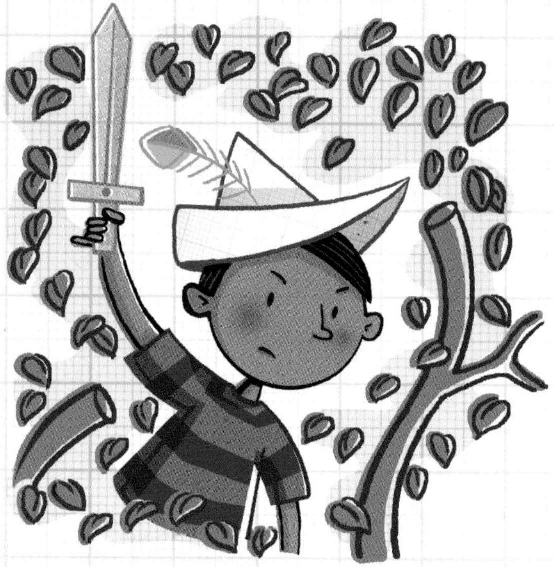

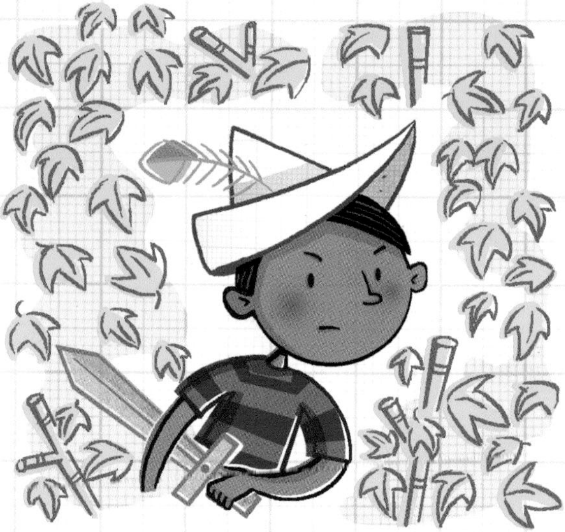

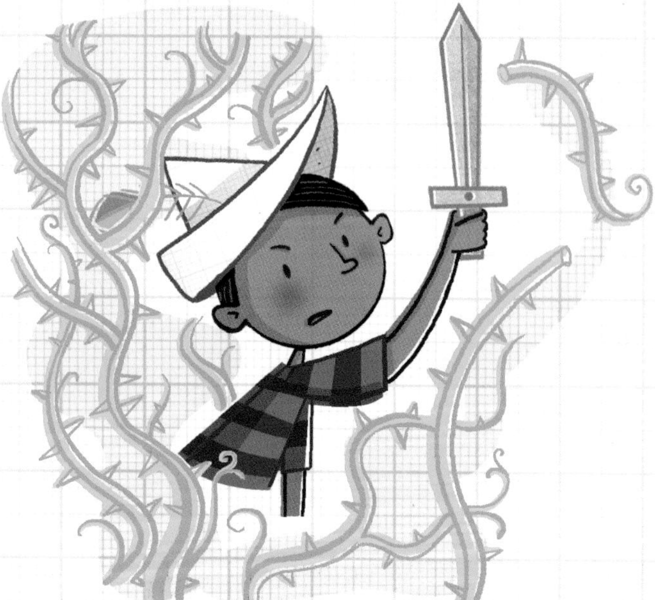

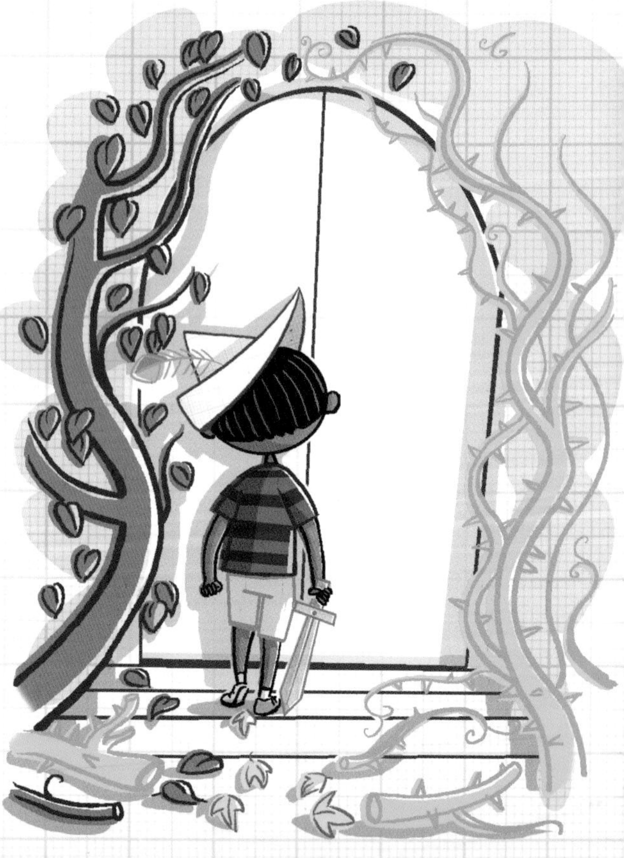

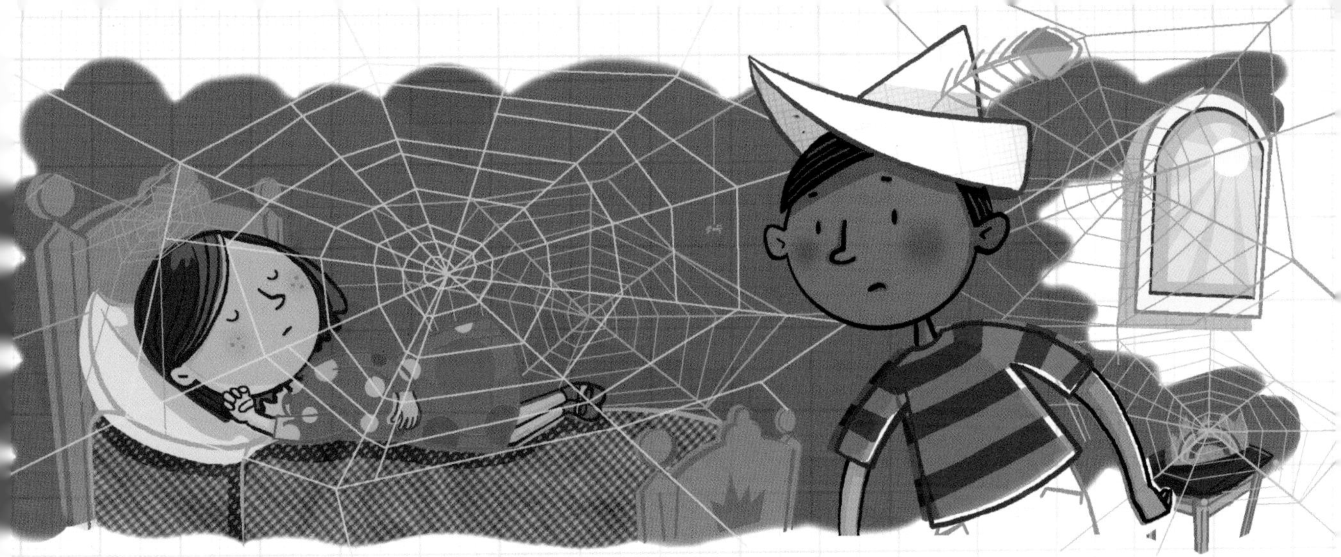

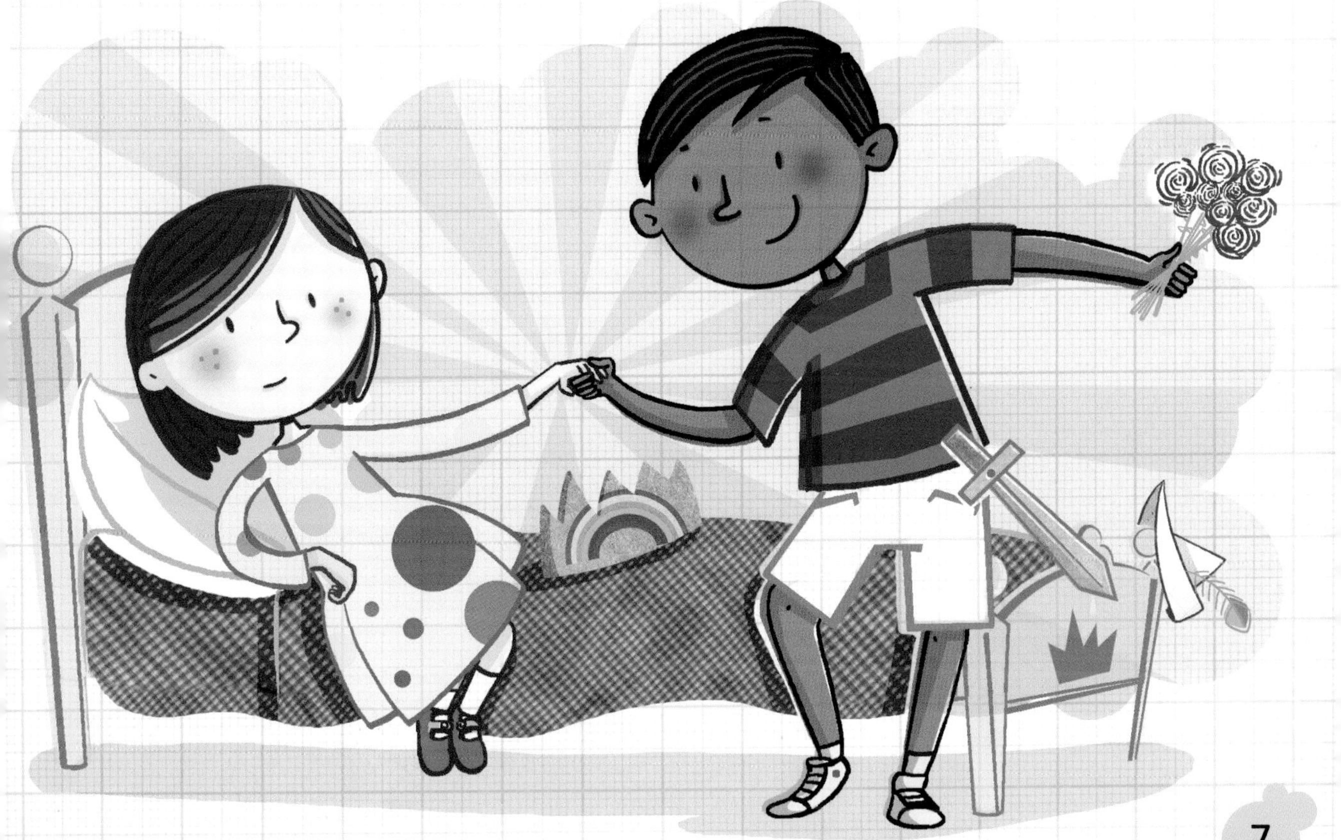

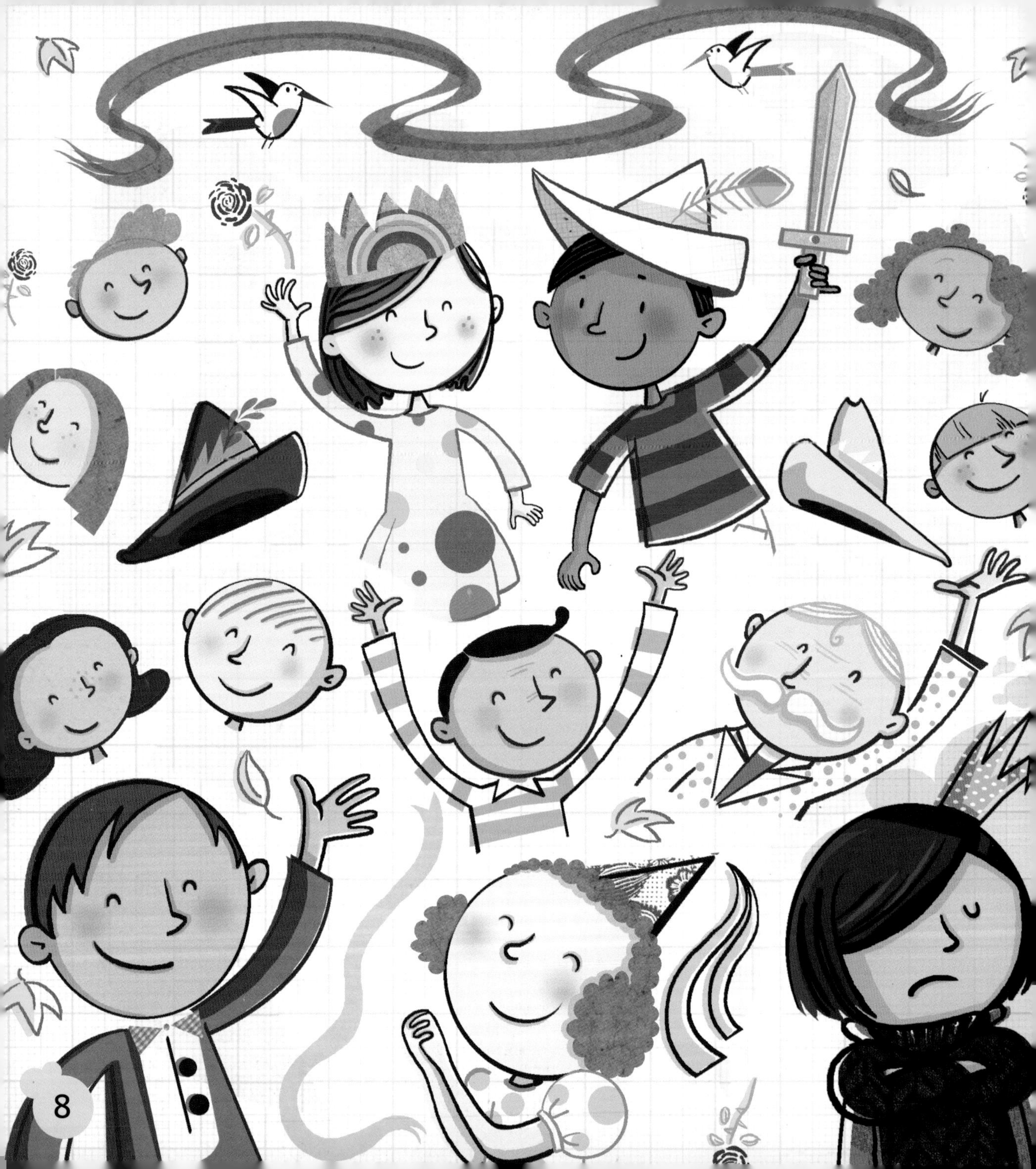